To Luke & Peter –
I hope this story inspires
you to dare to dream,
reach for the stars,
and know we CAN
get there!
Becky Cross

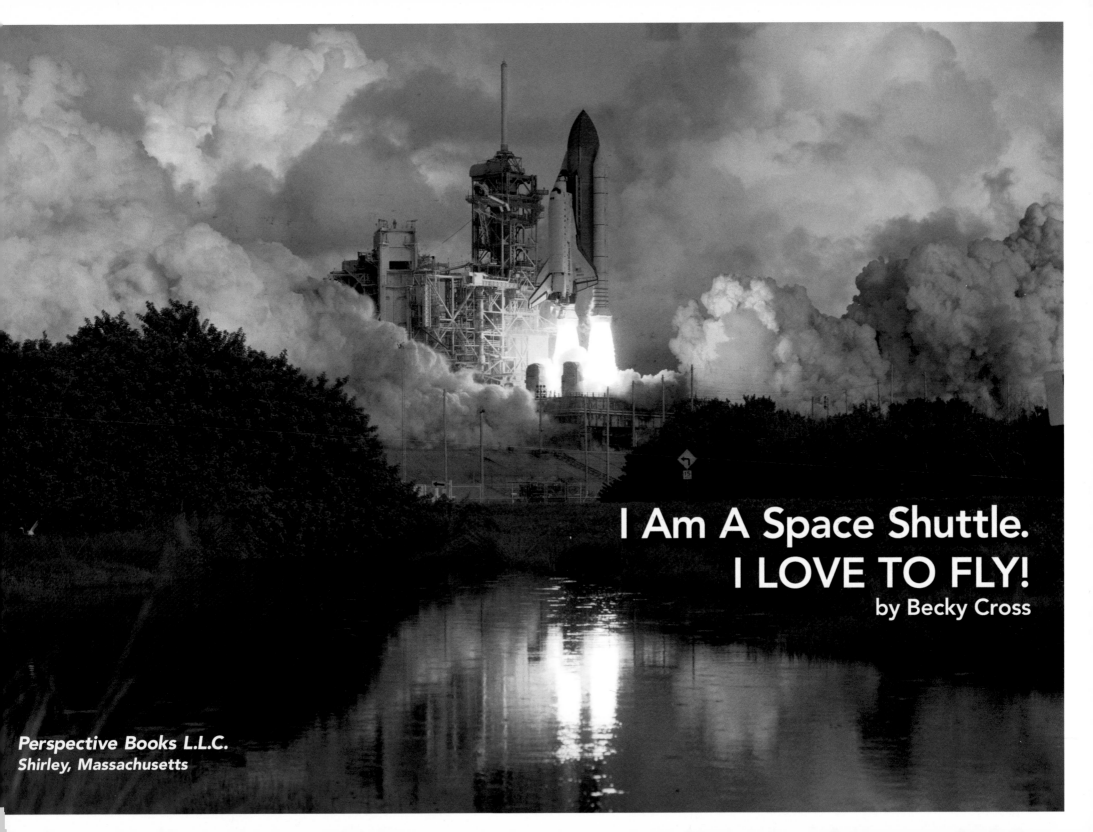

I Am A Space Shuttle.
I LOVE TO FLY!
by Becky Cross

Perspective Books L.L.C.
Shirley, Massachusetts

Art Direction: Becky Cross
Composition: Wendy Wetherbee

Perspective Books, LLC, P.O. Box 203, West Groton, MA 01472-0203

Library of Congress Card Number: 2003097373

ISBN 0-9701736-1-X

1 2 3 4 5 6 7 8 9 07 06 05 04 03   **Printed in Canada**

For my children, I hope that life's tragedies will not prevent you from following your dreams...

...in honor of all astronauts who despite the risk of tragedy follow their dreams anyway!

...with thanks to those who helped me fly....

Joe Parrish

Karen Barker

Margaret Persinger

Charlie Precourt

Bill Johnson

Tom Jones

Andy Chaikin

Julianne Zimmerman

Mike Gentry

Charles Tellier

...with special thanks to Jody Russell

I am a space shuttle.
I LOVE TO FLY!
I always look up
When I mount to the sky.

I zoom way up high
With no fear to look back;
I keep moving forward
With my *rocket launch pack*.

I take off in the sun
And sometimes in the dark,
Targeting each mission
For an 'in *orbit*' mark.

Yet I can't fly whenever
I feel the desire;
It takes time to prepare
To avoid a *misfire*.

So I'd rather they waited
And checked me all out
Than fly unprepared
And feel worry and doubt.

For the cargo I carry
Way up into space
Includes wonderful people
That you can NOT replace!

They have special duties
For each mission we fly.
It's amazing what we learn
When we're 200 miles high!

So I wait patiently
Through the steps that are needed,
So my return trips are safe
As the *checkout* is heeded.

It all started with a plan
For a ship to replace
The Saturn V rockets
That shot up into space.

Fortunately they had equipment
That was still lying around
That they decided could be useful
And might keep the price down!

They *refurbished* their buildings
And rebuilt what they had.
They still use the old *crawlers*,
The *platforms*, and *launch pad*.

And

They designed a new ship
That could be used many times,
Since 100 or so missions
Could save a few dimes!

9

So they began with just one
Carried high, piggyback,
Which they dropped from the sky
Testing its gliding down track.

And then they were ready
To send me to space
With two very brave men
Who were ready to face

The challenge!

We circled the Earth
For almost two days...
Outer space is so dark
You'd just be amazed!

11

We landed some distance
From our take off *locale*.
Then I piggybacked home
On my 747 pal.

And that's where it starts
With a plan called '*the flow*'.
From touchdown to touchdown
I am busy you know.

Getting up into space
Is no simple thing.
It takes two rocket boosters
And enough fuel for a king!

13

So to start....

When my crew leaves the runway,
I am checked through and through
To prevent *toxic* accidents,
It's something they MUST do!

14

Then I am towed to a place
That they call *OPF*.
It's three letters that mean
There's much more to do yet!

They built a big *scaffold*
So they can reach every inch
Of my outside and inside –
It's a rather tight pinch!

Thus I spend several months
While they poke and they prod.
It's like lubing your car or
Getting your horse *shod*.

You wouldn't want to travel
Without being quite sure
That everything is ship shape
And each system is pure.

They take me apart
From my stem to my stern.
They check EVERY system
And each part in its turn.

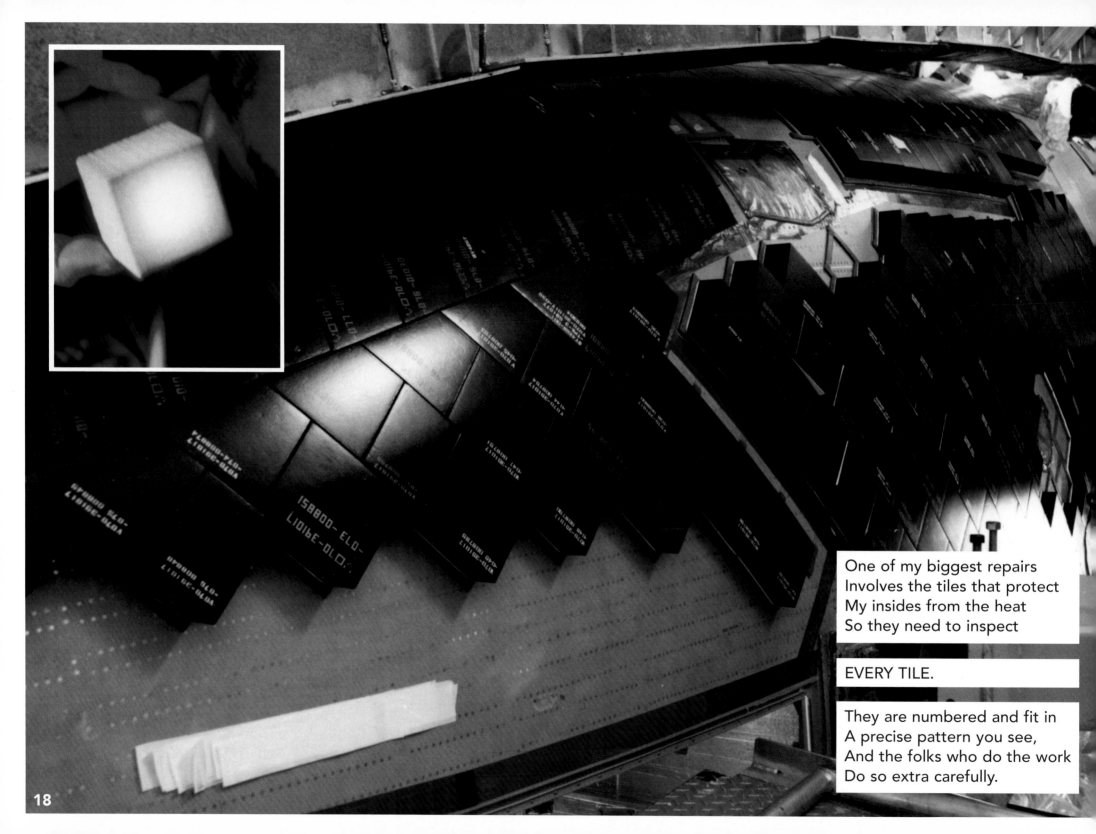

One of my biggest repairs
Involves the tiles that protect
My insides from the heat
So they need to inspect

EVERY TILE.

They are numbered and fit in
A precise pattern you see,
And the folks who do the work
Do so extra carefully.

I know that each person
Who works here tries hard,
With their heart and soul in it
And the kindest regard.

And when they are through
I am sent on my way,
But I know they'll be watching
My progress each day.

Then I'm towed to a building
They call the great *VAB*,
It is there that I am mated
To my partners: 1, 2, 3.

The VAB is immense;
It's over 500 feet.
It is the next part of the flow,
I'll be here at least a week.

Yet while I was being checked
On the outside and the in,
My two solid rocket boosters
Were prepared for our next spin.

After their fuel was *spent*
During their previous trip,
They gently dropped into the sea
For a long awaited dip.

They were towed in by two boats
(You might say that they'd been 'fished')
After which they were *inspected*,
Disassembled, and refurbished.

21

Later on they are brought here
To be built up off the floor
On the platform from which we'll launch
After traveling out the door.

Next comes the orange fuel tank.
Its designers just might boast
That it is brought by barge to NASA
From the Louisiana coast.

They hoist it to the platform
Between the *SRBs*.
Its massive *hulk* is *vacuous*
In feet it's 1-5-3.

24

When I arrive they are ready
To hoist me up in the air.
They attach a giant harness
Using caution and every care.

They lift me into the rafters.
Then I glide like silk toward my pals.
The trip may take several hours,
But it ends in a '*stack*' totale!

A stack is what we are together.
Each piece can do nothing alone.
But each of us is a team player
With the 100 or so missions we've flown.

Then once each bolt has been tightened,
And every seal has been checked for leaks,
A crawler is moved in beneath us
To go to the pad for a few weeks.

The crawler moves like molasses.
It avoids the slightest of shakes.
With a top speed of one mile an hour,
You should see the size of its brakes!

It drives us out to the launch pad
Where it slowly backs away.
Once the crawler leaves the platform,
The **RSS** moves into play.

It acts as a kind of cover
That protects me from the wind.
It moves on a track on rollers
'Til it stops and I am pinned.

It's not only there to protect me.
It also allows them to touch
The *payload* traveling with me
Up to the last hours before launch.

29

Hours before we get going,
The crew climbs in through my hatch.
The staff hangs out in the **white room**.
They are the last minute dispatch.

But once my guests are settled,
The RSS sets me free.
We sit tight on the launch pad
Awaiting commands launch plea.

The countdown clicks on a view screen
As they check each system again.
We sit awaiting the launch call
Thinking of time that we will spend

Up in space!

At '7' my engines start burning
As water muffles the sound.
After count '1' we are released
And moving off the ground.

Then we REALLY start moving
Like a bullet shot from a gun.
The fuel burns off in minutes,
The SRBs and tank are done!

Once up, our mission begins.
Each time is different you see.
New teams are always training
For the launches yet to be.

We ALL have to look forward,
Or things will not improve.
Back at the NASA centers
Engineers are on the move.

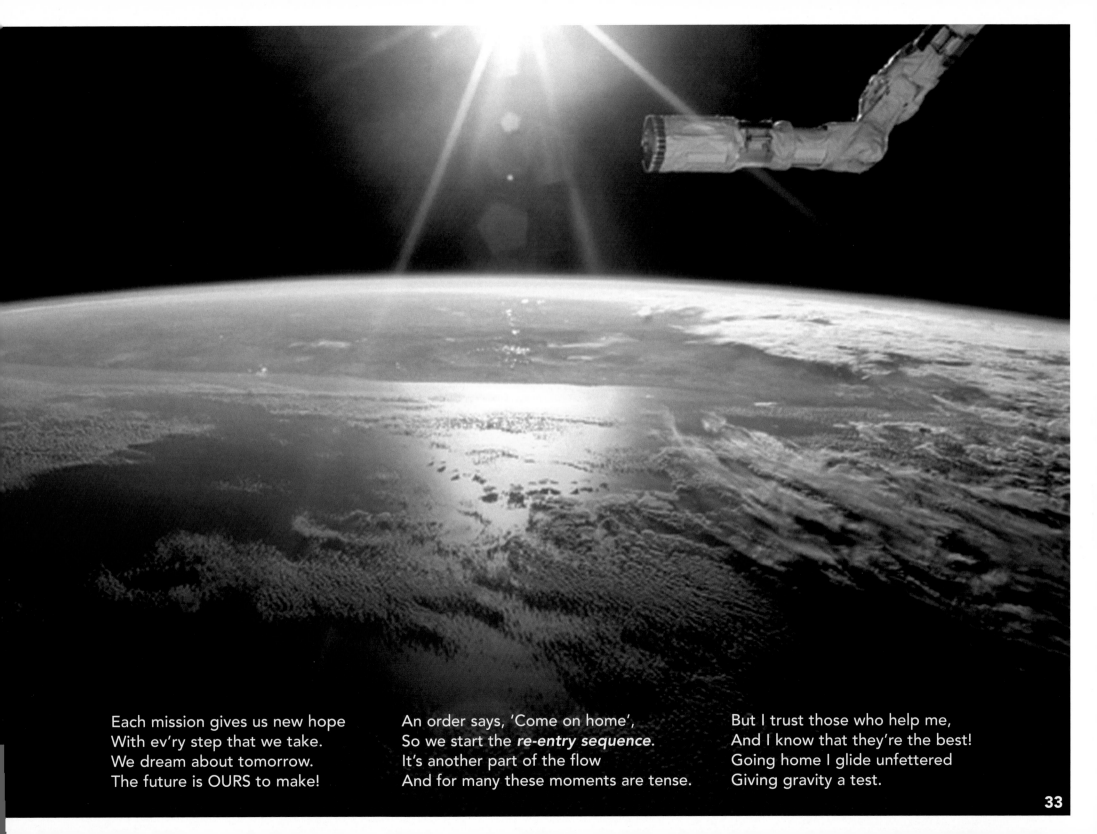

Each mission gives us new hope
With ev'ry step that we take.
We dream about tomorrow.
The future is OURS to make!

An order says, 'Come on home',
So we start the *re-entry sequence*.
It's another part of the flow
And for many these moments are tense.

But I trust those who help me,
And I know that they're the best!
Going home I glide unfettered
Giving gravity a test.

Double *booms* tell of our coming
To those who wait on the ground.
Like drums signal victory,
Hopeful ears can't wait for the sound!

34

My rear wheels always touch first,
The ground that we've all missed.
Space is a lifetime adventure,
But coming home to Earth is bliss!

And that is where it all starts
With a plan we call 'the flow'.
From touchdown to next touchdown
I'll be busy, now YOU know!

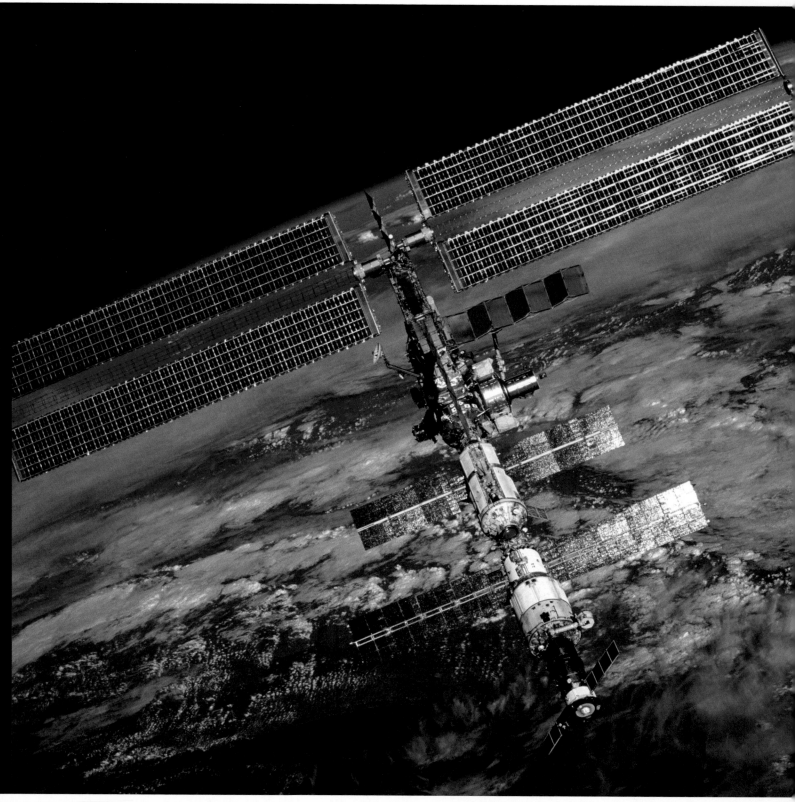

Glossary

Booms: Sonic booms. When the orbiter crosses the sound barrier (slows down to around 600 mph) it makes a loud noise that can be heard from far away, even on the ground.

Checkout: steps taken for a thorough inspection

Crawler: a machine that picks up and carries the mobile launch platform and the space shuttle stack to and from the launch pad.

Disassemble: take apart very carefully

Flow, or 'the flow': the series of steps taken to safely process the space shuttle for its missions in space.

'From my stem to my stern': an expression that means from the very front to the very back.

Hulk: shell, the outside 'skin'

Inspect: look over very carefully

Launch pad: the area where rockets are launched into space.

Locale: place, location

Misfire: malfunction, breakdown, failure

OPF: Orbiter Processing Facility, a building designed specifically for engineers to work on space shuttle orbiters after they return from space and before they are attached to the rest of the stack in the VAB prior to launch.

Orbit: a flight path that completely circles the Earth

Payload: scientific experiments, supplies, and equipment carried up into space.

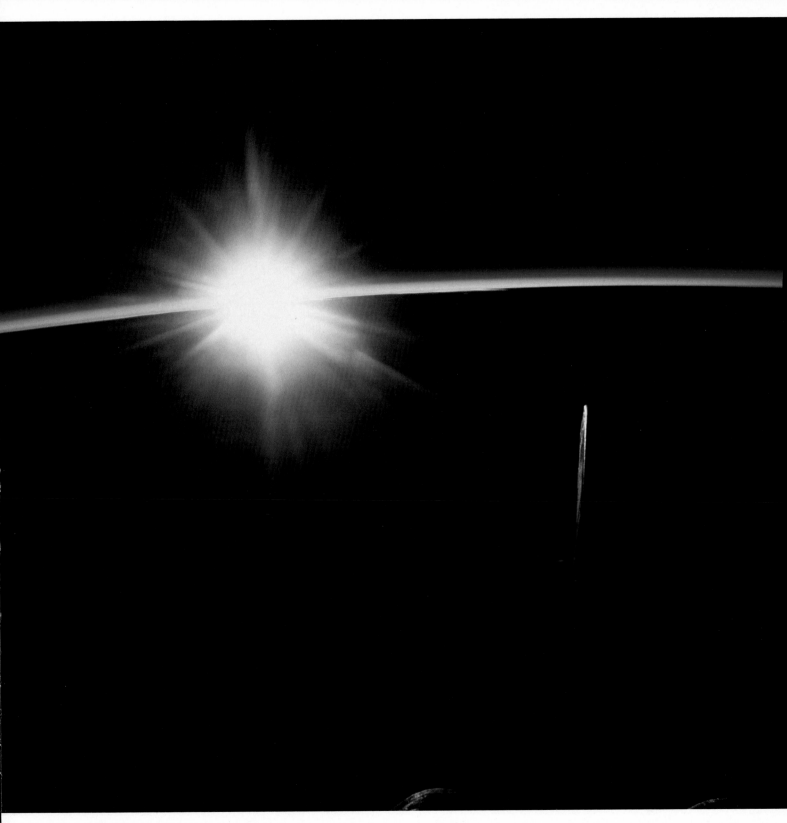

Platform: a raised area on which the space shuttle stack is connected and from which it will launch.

Re-entry sequence: the ordered list of tasks that astronauts must do before the return to Earth.

Refurbish: restore, fix up

'Rocket launch pack': the two SRBs and the external fuel tank.

RSS: Rotating Service Structure, part of the building at the launch pad that moves back and forth over the space shuttle in final preparation for launch.

Scaffold: : a structure built to completely surround space shuttle orbiters to make it easier for engineers to work on them.

Shod: the process of removing old horseshoes; cleaning, trimming, and caring for the horse's feet; and putting new horseshoes on the horse's hooves.

Spent: used up

SRBs: Solid Rocket Boosters, two white rockets alongside the space shuttle orbiter that help put it into orbit.

Stack: a space shuttle stack is made up of four pieces: the space shuttle orbiter, two solid rocket boosters, and the orange external fuel tank.

Toxic: poisonous, contaminated

VAB: Vehicle Assembly Building, the large building where among other things the space shuttle stack is assembled.

Vacuous: very roomy, spacious, a large empty space.

White Room: a room that is kept very clean through which the astronauts board the space shuttle.

Image List

Hosting location of image is listed in parentheses

DFRC images can be found at: http://www.dfrc.nasa.gov
JSC images can be viewed at: http://spaceflight.nasa.gov
For those not on the web please call: (281) 483-4231
KSC images can be viewed at: http://images.ksc.nasa.gov
MSFC images can be found at: http://mix.msfc.nasa.gov
SSC images can be found at: http://www.ssc.nasa.gov
Additional searches can be done through the NASA Image
Exchange (NIX) website http://nix.nasa.gov and the Great
Images in NASA site: http://grin.hq.nasa.gov

Most but not all of the images contained in this book can be
found at the sites listed above since the author did extensive
searches with the assistance of the image librarian at JSC
through multiple sites. This list of links, however, will provide
the reader with a large collection to view and download.

Please also check our website for further information as it
becomes available www.perspectivebooks.com